THIS IS A *beautiful* RECORD OF

God's Love

IN THE LIFE OF:

o . . . . o

o . . . . o

o . . . . o

A
beautiful
Bible Study

A Season of Sowing

8-Week Bible Study Guide and Prayer Journal

Other Bible Studies by Heather Carr

The Book of James: 5-Week Women's Bible Study and Prayer Journal

Take Heart: 31-Day Bible Reading Plan and Prayer Journal

Praying the Promises: 21-Day Scripture Writing Plan and Prayer Journal

A Season of Sowing Bible Study Guide and Prayer Journal
© 2018 by Heather Carr

ISBN-13: 978-1722128234

ISBN-10: 1722128232

Requests for information should be addressed to:
Heather@HeatherKernickCarr.com

Table of Contents

A Note from Heather

Welcome to the Beautiful Bible Studies A Season of Sowing Bible Study. I created this Bible study guide and prayer journal to help us learn how to depend on God to direct our daily lives. I believe the key to living a life filled with purpose, joy and satisfaction is walking in obedience to God through intimate prayer time and study time in His Word.

It's my hope and prayer that this study will help you draw near to God, renew your mind through the study of His Word and discover the next step in your journey with God. To get the most out of this study, I encourage you to join our online Bible Study community for women, where you'll find encouragement for your journey, coloring pages created to help you meditate on the truths found in these pages and a wonderful group of Christian women to share the journey with you.

As you make your way through this study, I'd love to hear what you are thinking and what God is speaking to you through his Word. To join in the conversation, visit me and a group of beautiful, Jesus-loving women like you at BeautifulBibleStudies.com.

Much love,

Heather

1. Gather Your Supplies. You'll need:

- This journal

- A Bible or two (I like to use an NIV Study Bible and an ESV Bible)

- A pen or pencil in whatever colors make you happy

- A blank notebook or journal (if you are reading an electronic copy of this study)

2. The Daily Routine. Each day for the next 21 days we'll:

- Write out the daily scripture

- Proclaim the Word over our lives with a daily affirmation

- Write a prayer using the prayer prompts provided

- Record at least one thing you are thankful to God for in your life

3. Frequently Asked Questions. Just in case you're wondering:

- *What if I fall behind?* No worries. Go at your own pace. If you need a day off or want to spread the daily routine over a couple of days, no problem.

- *How long will this take?* The daily routine can take as little as 10 minutes or as long as a half an hour or more, depending on your availability and what you hope to gain from of it. There's no right or wrong amount of time, as long as you're spending time with God in His Word.

- *Can I ask you a question?* Yes! Send your question to me at Heather@HeatherKernickCarr.com. I love hearing from you, but I'm a mom to three, so please give me a day or two to get back with you.

- *Will you pray for me?* Yes! Join us at BeautifulBibleStudies.com to submit your prayer request or send me an email. I'm honored to personally pray over each and every request I receive.

Woe to me! I cried. I am ruined! For I am a man of unclean lips, and I live among a people of unclean lips, and my eyes have seen the King, the Lord Almighty.

Isaiah 6:5

CHAPTER 1

Preparing the Soil

Preparing the Soil

Write Hosea 10:12 in the space below.

....

....

....

....

....

....

....

....

....

....

....

....

....

....

Record one word or phrase that stands out to you.

....

....

....

....

What might God be saying to me?

···
···
···
···
···
···
···
···
···
···

What might God be telling me to do?

···
···
···
···
···
···
···
···
···
···

Preparing the Soil

PRAYER

Write a prayer asking the Lord to give you ears to hear His voice.

Write Proverbs 28:13 in the space below.

Record one word or phrase that stands out to you.

Preparing the Soil

What might God be saying to me?

....

....

....

....

....

....

....

....

....

....

What might God be telling me to do?

....

....

....

....

....

....

....

....

....

....

PRAYER

Ask the Father to reveal any sins you may be concealing from Him or yourself. Confess them below.

Preparing the Soil

Read Psalm 51.

Record one word or phrase that stands out to you.

....

....

....

....

What might God be saying to me?

....

....

....

....

....

....

....

What might God be telling me to do?

....

....

....

....

....

....

PRAYER

Thank and praise God for creating a clean heart inside of you. Ask Him to give you the words to speak savation into someone's life today.

Preparing the Soil

Read Luke 13:1-9.

Record one word or phrase that stands out to you.

....

....

....

....

What might God be saying to me?

....

....

....

....

....

....

What might God be telling me to do?

....

....

....

....

....

....

PRAYER

Ask the Father to plant you in good soil. Listen for a minute, then record any thoughts that come into your mind.

Pray over these thoughts.

Preparing the Soil

....

Read Isaiah 6:1-8.

Record one word or phrase that stands out to you.

....

....

....

....

What might God be saying to me?

....

....

....

....

....

....

....

What might God be telling me to do?

....

....

....

....

....

....

PRAYER

Ask God to reveal to you anything holding you back from the plan He has for your life. Write out a prayer
addressing any setbacks He reveals to you and asking Him to send you out on a mission for His kingdom.

Preparing the Soil

Finding Your Calling Exercise: Confess any fears, doubts or insecurities that are blocking your ability to live each day fully available to God's call.

LIVING A LIFE OF PURPOSE

Have I not commanded you?

Be strong and courageous.

Do not be afraid; do not be discouraged,

for the Lord your God will be with you

wherever you go.

Joshua 1:9

THOUGHTS

....
....
....
....
....
....
....
....
....
....
....
....

QUESTIONS

....
....
....
....
....
....
....
....
....
....
....
....

PREPARE
to *share*

FAVORITES

....
....
....
....
....
....
....
....
....
....
....
....

PRAYER NEEDS

....
....
....
....
....
....
....
....
....
....
....
....

TWO ARE BETTER
than **ONE**

PRAYER

Write a prayer for your small group, Sunday school class or our online community. Ask that the Lord be honored through your conversation and fellowship time together.

REST & REFLECT

A verse to meditate on this week: If we confess our sins, he is

faithful and just and will forgive us our sins and purify us from all

unrighteousness.. 1 John 1:9

Preparing the Soil

Suggested Flow: Opening Prayer, Read Scripture, Review Prepare to Share Notes, Watch Video, Discuss Questions, Closing Prayer

1. What does it mean to repent?

2. Why do you think repentance is important?

3. What does it look like to live with the joy of salvation?

4. What does it mean to have a willing spirit?

5. What do you think the Parable of the Fig Tree means?

6 . Why do you think it is sometimes hard for people to repent?

7. Why do you think it was important that Isaiah's sin be atoned for before he was sent out to deliver God's message?

8. What is the relationship between repentance and having a willing spirit? How does this effect our ability to live out God's purpose for our lives?

The light shines in the darkness, and the darkness has not overcome it.

John 1:5

CHAPTER 2
In the Dark

In the Dark

Write Ecclesiastes 11:6 in the space below.

....

....

....

....

....

....

....

....

....

....

....

....

....

....

....

Record one word or phrase that stands out to you.

....

....

....

....

What might God be saying to me?

....

....

....

....

....

....

....

....

....

....

....

What might God be telling me to do?

....

....

....

....

....

....

....

....

....

....

PRAYER

Write a prayer asking God to help you trust in His knowledge instead of your own.

Write Proverbs 2:1-5 in the space below.

Record one word or phrase that stands out to you.

In the Dark

What might God be saying to me?

....
....
....
....
....
....
....
....
....
....

What might God be telling me to do?

....
....
....
....
....
....
....
....
....

PRAYER

Write a prayer calling out to God for wisdom and understanding.

In the Dark

Read Psalm 130.

Record one word or phrase that stands out to you.

....

....

....

....

What might God be saying to me?

....

....

....

....

....

....

What might God be telling me to do?

....

....

....

....

....

PRAYER

Write a prayer asking God to help you wait on Him. List any specific areas in your life in which you need help persevering with patience.

In the Dark

Read Matthew 13:31-32.

Record one word or phrase that stands out to you.

....

....

....

....

What might God be saying to me?

....

....

....

....

....

....

....

....

What might God be telling me to do?

....

....

....

....

....

....

PRAYER

Record a prayer thanking God for giving you a place of refuge in Him.

In the Dark

○ .... ○

Read 1 Samuel 1:1-28.

Record one word or phrase that stands out to you.

....

....

....

....

What might God be saying to me?

....

....

....

....

....

....

....

What might God be telling me to do?

....

....

....

....

....

....

PRAYER

Ask the Lord to help you pour out your soul to Him. Record a prayer leaving your deepest desires in God's hands.

In the Dark

Living a life of purpose requires trust in God's plan. Ask the Lord to make the desires of your heart line up with His plan for you. Sit for a minute and listen for His response. Record your thoughts below.

LIVING A LIFE OF PURPOSE

Day Five

The Lord has granted me
what I asked of him.

1 Samuel 1:27

THOUGHTS

....
....
....
....
....
....
....
....
....
....
....
....

QUESTIONS

....
....
....
....
....
....
....
....
....
....
....

PREPARE
to *share*

FAVORITES

....
....
....
....
....
....
....
....
....
....
....
....

PRAYER NEEDS

....
....
....
....
....
....
....
....
....
....
....

TWO *are better than* ONE

PRAYER

Write a prayer for your small group, Sunday school class or our online community. Ask that the Lord be honored through your conversation and fellowship time together.

REST & REFLECT

A verse to meditate on this week: He will also send you rain for the seed you sow in the ground, and the food that comes from the land will be rich and plentiful. In that day your cattle will graze in broad meadows. Isaiah 30:23

In the Dark

1. Have you ever experienced a time in your life in which it felt as if God left you in the dark? Were you able to trust Him eve when you didn't understand?

2. What do you think it means to seek after wsdom? Why is this important today?

3. What is the relationship between forgiveness, waiting and hope?

4. What does redemption mean to you?

5. Good things take time to grow and mature. Is there any area of your life in which you are rushing ahead, instead of allowing God to refine and mature your spirit?

6 . How do you make time to rest in God's presence? Do you think this practice is important?

7. What is the one thing you desire most in the world? Are you willing to hand it back to God like Hannah did?

8. What does it mean to you to wait expectantly for God to grant the desires of your heart?

He must become greater, I must become less.

John 3:30

CHAPTER 3
Breaking Open

Breaking Open

Write John 12:23-24 in the space below.

....

....

....

....

....

....

....

....

....

....

....

....

....

....

Record one word or phrase that stands out to you.

....

....

....

....

What might God be saying to me?

....

....

....

....

....

....

....

....

....

....

What might God be telling me to do?

....

....

....

....

....

....

....

....

....

PRAYER

Write a prayer asking God to help you let go of the things you believe about yourself: your abilities and strengths, insecurities and weaknesses so that His power can increase in you.

....

....

....

....

....

....

....

....

....

....

....

....

....

....

....

....

....

....

....

Write Proverbs 3:5-6 in the space below.

Record one word or phrase that stands out to you.

Breaking Open

What might God be saying to me?

···
···
···
···
···
···
···
···
···
···

What might God be telling me to do?

···
···
···
···
···
···
···
···
···

PRAYER

Ask the Lord to reveal to you any ways in which you are relying on yourself instead of Him. Sit quietly and listen for His response. Record your thoughts below.

Breaking Open

Read Psalm 132.

Record one word or phrase that stands out to you.

....

....

....

....

What might God be saying to me?

....

....

....

....

....

....

....

What might God be telling me to do?

....

....

....

....

....

....

PRAYER

Write a prayer asking the Lord to help you put Him above all else in your life, even your own comfort.

Breaking Open

Read Matthew 13:44-46.

Record one word or phrase that stands out to you.

....

....

....

....

What might God be saying to me?

....

....

....

....

....

....

....

What might God be telling me to do?

....

....

....

....

....

....

PRAYER

Write a prayer asking the Lord to help you understand how valuable His kingdom truly is and to give you a heart willing to give all you have in exchange for what matters most to Him.

Breaking Open

Read Esther 4:1-17.

Record one word or phrase that stands out to you.

....

....

....

....

What might God be saying to me?

....

....

....

....

....

....

....

What might God be telling me to do?

....

....

....

....

....

....

PRAYER

Write a prayer of intercession for someone you know. Ask God to help him or her have the courage to live according to God's plan and purpose.

Breaking Open

What breaks your heart? Make a list of things that make your heartache such as hunger, homelessness or orphaned children. What problems are people facing that you desperately wish you could change?

LIVING A LIFE OF PURPOSE

Yet who knows whether you have come to the kingdom for such a time as this?

Esther 4:14

THOUGHTS

·····························
·····························
·····························
·····························
·····························
·····························
·····························
·····························
·····························
·····························
·····························
·····························

QUESTIONS

·····························
·····························
·····························
·····························
·····························
·····························
·····························
·····························
·····························
·····························
·····························
·····························

PREPARE
to *share*

FAVORITES

·····························
·····························
·····························
·····························
·····························
·····························
·····························
·····························
·····························
·····························
·····························
·····························

PRAYER NEEDS

·····························
·····························
·····························
·····························
·····························
·····························
·····························
·····························
·····························
·····························
·····························
·····························

TWO *ARE BETTER*
than ONE

Day Six

PRAYER

Write a prayer for your small group, Sunday school class or our online community. Ask that the Lord be honored through your conversation and fellowship time together.

REST & REFLECT

A verse to meditate on this week: Your kingdom come,

your will be done, on earth as it is in heaven. Matthew 6:10

Breaking Open

1. What do you think it means to "produce many seeds"?

2. How might our understanding of our strengths and weaknesses hinder us from doing the work God created us to do?

3. What does it mean to you to acknowledge God in all your ways?

4. How do you know if you are depending on god or depending on yourself to accomplish a task?

5. Why do you think self-denial is so difficult to embrace in our culture?

6 . In what ways is the Lord calling you to deny yourself in order to make room for Him to dwell in your heart?

7. Why do you think Jesus compares the kingdom of God to a hidden treasure?

8. Esther said yes to God's call on her life, even though she knew it could cosr her everything. When was the last time you took a risk to say yes to God?

I have come into the world as a light, so that no one who believes in me should stay in darkness. John 12:46

CHAPTER 4

Born Into the Light

Born Into the Light

Write Mark 4:26-29 in the space below.

....

....

....

....

....

....

....

....

....

....

....

....

....

....

Record one word or phrase that stands out to you.

....

....

....

....

What might God be saying to me?

....

....

....

....

....

....

....

....

....

....

What might God be telling me to do?

....

....

....

....

....

....

....

....

....

....

PRAYER

Write a prayer asking God to help you let go of the need to understand everything and trust that He will create something beautiful and meaningful out of the one life you've been given.

Write Proverbs 19:23 in the space below.

Record one word or phrase that stands out to you.

Born Into the Light

What might God be saying to me?

....

....

....

....

....

....

....

....

....

What might God be telling me to do?

....

....

....

....

....

....

....

....

....

PRAYER

Write a prayer thanking God for His protection. Ask Him to help you fully believe you are safe and secure with Him.

Born Into the Light

Read Psalm 104.

Record one word or phrase that stands out to you.

....

....

....

....

What might God be saying to me?

....

....

....

....

....

....

What might God be telling me to do?

....

....

....

....

....

....

PRAYER

Spend some time observing nature this morning. Write a prayer of praise to God for the wonders He has created in the world and in you.

Born Into the Light

Read John 3:1-21.

Record one word or phrase that stands out to you.

....

....

....

....

What might God be saying to me?

....

....

....

....

....

....

....

....

What might God be telling me to do?

....

....

....

....

....

....

PRAYER

Write a prayer thanking and praising God for His great love for you.

Born Into the Light

Read Acts 9:1-31.

Record one word or phrase that stands out to you.

....

....

....

....

What might God be saying to me?

....

....

....

....

....

....

....

What might God be telling me to do?

....

....

....

....

....

....

PRAYER

Ask God how you can say yes to His call this week. Sit quietly for a moment and listen for His response. Record your thoughts below.

Born Into the Light

Review the list you created last week on page 61. Create a list of existing ministries or nonprofit organizations already working on these issues either locally or globally.

LIVING A LIFE OF PURPOSE

Day Five

For God so loved the world that he gave his one and only Son, that whoever believes in him shall not perish but have eternal life.

John 3:16

THOUGHTS

....
....
....
....
....
....
....
....
....
....
....
....

QUESTIONS

....
....
....
....
....
....
....
....
....
....
....
....

PREPARE
to share

FAVORITES

....
....
....
....
....
....
....
....
....
....
....
....

PRAYER NEEDS

....
....
....
....
....
....
....
....
....
....
....
....

TWO ARE BETTER
than ONE

PRAYER

Write a prayer for your small group, Sunday school class or our online community. Ask that the Lord be honored through your conversation and fellowship time together.

REST & REFLECT

A verse to meditate on this week: Do not conform to the pattern of this world, but be transformed by the renewing of your mind. Then you will be able to test and approve what God's will is—his good, pleasing and perfect will. Romans 12:2

Born Into the Light

Suggested Flow: *Opening Prayer, Read Scripture, Review Prepare to Share Notes, Watch Video, Discuss Questions, Closing Prayer*

1. How has your life changed since you began following Jesus?

2. Were you always aware of the changes taking place in your heart?

3. What do you think it means to "rest untouched by trouble" (Proverbs 19:23)?

4. Is the meditation of your heart and mind pleasing to God? Why or why not?

5. Do you think it's possible to fully understand the love God has for you? Why or why not?

6 . What do you think it means to live by the truth?

7. How might Saul's story be different if Ananias and Barnabas had said no to God's call?

8. How might our story be different if Saul had said no to Jesus' plan for his life?

"I, Jesus, have sent my angel to give
you this testimony for the churches.
I am the Root and the Offspring of
David, and the bright Morning Star."

Revelation 22:16

CHAPTER 5
Taking Root

Taking Root

Write Jeremiah 17:7-8 in the space below.

Record one word or phrase that stands out to you.

What might God be saying to me?

....
....
....
....
....
....
....
....
....
....

What might God be telling me to do?

....
....
....
....
....
....
....
....
....

PRAYER

Write a prayer asking God to plant your life where you will never fail to bear fruit for His kingdom.

Write Proverbs 12:12 in the space below.

....

....

....

....

....

....

....

....

....

....

....

....

....

....

....

Record one word or phrase that stands out to you.

....

....

....

....

....

Taking Root

What might God be saying to me?

....

....

....

....

....

....

....

....

....

....

What might God be telling me to do?

....

....

....

....

....

....

....

....

....

PRAYER

Ask the Father to help you understand what it means to be rooted in righteousness. Sit quietly and listen for His reply. Record your thoughts below.

Taking Root

Read Psalm 1.

Record one word or phrase that stands out to you.

....

....

....

....

What might God be saying to me?

....

....

....

....

....

....

What might God be telling me to do?

....

....

....

....

....

....

PRAYER

Write a prayer thanking and praising God for His Word. Ask the Father to give you a heart that delights in His Word.

Taking Root

Read Matthew 13:3-23.

Record one word or phrase that stands out to you.

....

....

....

....

What might God be saying to me?

....

....

....

....

....

....

....

What might God be telling me to do?

....

....

....

....

....

....

PRAYER

Wrtie a prayer asking the Lord to help you hear the Word and understand it.

Taking Root

Read 1 Kings 19:7-13.

Record one word or phrase that stands out to you.

....

....

....

....

What might God be saying to me?

....

....

....

....

....

....

....

What might God be telling me to do?

....

....

....

....

....

....

PRAYER

Write out a prayer asking the Lord to give you eyes to see Him, ears to hear Him and a heart that understands what He is calling you to do.

Pray over each of the ministries you listed last week. Ask the Lord to reveal to you how you can be a part of the work He is doing in the world. Listen for His response. Record your thoughts here.

LIVING A LIFE OF PURPOSE

And after the fire came a gentle whisper.

1 Kings 20:12

THOUGHTS

·························
·························
·························
·························
·························
·························
·························
·························
·························
·························
·························
·························
·························
·························
·························

PREPARE
to *share*

QUESTIONS

·························
·························
·························
·························
·························
·························
·························
·························
·························
·························
·························
·························
·························
·························
·························

FAVORITES

·························
·························
·························
·························
·························
·························
·························
·························
·························
·························
·························
·························
·························
·························
·························

TWO *ARE BETTER*
than ONE

PRAYER NEEDS

·························
·························
·························
·························
·························
·························
·························
·························
·························
·························
·························
·························
·························
·························
·························

PRAYER

Write a prayer for your small group, Sunday school class or our online community. Ask that the Lord be honored through your conversation and fellowship time together.

REST & REFLECT

A verse to meditate on this week: So then, just as you received Christ Jesus as Lord, continue to live your lives in him, rooted and built up in him, strengthened in the faith as you were taught, and overflowing with thankfulness. Colossians 2:6-7

Taking Root

1. What does it mean to bear fruit for God's kingdom?

2. Whhat does it look like to live a life rooted in righteousness?

3. How does delighting in God's Word change our perspective?

4. What does the seed falling on good soil refer to?

5. Have you ever heard the gentle whisper of God speak to your heart? Share your experience.

6 . God asks Elijah, "What are you doing here?" How would you answer if God asked the same of you?

7. How does a life rooted in Christ lead to a heart overflowing with thankfulness?

8. In what ways have you said 'yes' to God this week? How did you hear His voice? What was your response?

He said to him, "In my dream I saw a vine in front of me, and on the vine were three branches. As soon as it budded, it blossomed, and its clusters ripened into grapes."

Genesis 40:9-10

CHAPTER 6

Budding Faith

Budding Faith

Write Matthew 24:32 in the space below.

....

....

....

....

....

....

....

....

....

....

....

....

....

....

....

Record one word or phrase that stands out to you.

....

....

....

....

What might God be saying to me?

....
....
....
....
....
....
....
....
....
....

What might God be telling me to do?

....
....
....
....
....
....
....
....
....
....

PRAYER

Write a prayer thanking God for all the seasons of you life. Ask Him to help you recognize His will for you today.

Write Proverbs 10:31 in the space below.

....

....

....

....

....

....

....

....

....

....

....

....

....

....

....

....

Record one word or phrase that stands out to you.

....

....

....

....

....

Budding Faith

What might God be saying to me?

....

....

....

....

....

....

....

....

....

....

What might God be telling me to do?

....

....

....

....

....

....

....

....

....

PRAYER

Write a prayer asking God to bless your speech with the fruit of wisdom.

Budding Faith

Read Psalm 32.

Record one word or phrase that stands out to you.

....

....

....

....

What might God be saying to me?

....

....

....

....

....

....

What might God be telling me to do?

....

....

....

....

....

PRAYER

Rejoice and be glad! Write a prayer of praise and thanksgiving to the Lord.

Budding Faith

Read Luke 11:5-10.

Record one word or phrase that stands out to you.

....

....

....

....

What might God be saying to me?

....

....

....

....

....

....

....

What might God be telling me to do?

....

....

....

....

....

....

PRAYER

Write a prayer asking God to help you understand His purpose for your life. Thank Him for answering you.

Budding Faith

Read Exodus 4:1-17; 29-31.

Record one word or phrase that stands out to you.

....

....

....

....

What might God be saying to me?

....

....

....

....

....

....

What might God be telling me to do?

....

....

....

....

....

....

PRAYER

Write a prayer asking God to help you trust and obey Him, even when you feel inadequate.

Budding Faith

What makes your heart rejoice? Make a list of things you deeply enjoy doing.

LIVING A LIFE OF PURPOSE

Now go, I will help you speak and will teach you what to say.

Exodus 4:12

THOUGHTS

QUESTIONS

PREPARE
to share

FAVORITES

PRAYER NEEDS

TWO ARE BETTER
than ONE

PRAYER

Write a prayer for your small group, Sunday school class or our online community. Ask that the Lord be honored through your conversation and fellowship time together.

REST & REFLECT

A verse to meditate on this week: Call to me and I will answer you and tell you great and unsearchable things you do not know. Jeremiah 33:3

Budding Faith

Suggested Flow: Opening Prayer, Read Scripture, Review Prepare to Share Notes, Watch Video, Discuss Questions, Closing Prayer

1. What are some signs you experience in your life when God is trying to communicate with you?

2. How do you know it's God speaking and instructing you?

3. What is the fruit of wisdom?

4. Do you think singing is an important component to a healthy relationship with God? Why or why not?

5. What's your favorite hymn or worship song right now? Why?

6 . What is something you're seeking after God for right now?

7.Why do you think Moses wanted God to send someone else? Have you ever made excuses instead of being obedient to God's call?

8. In what ways have you said 'yes' to God this week? How did you hear His voice? What was your response?

For, before the harvest, when the blossom is gone

and the flower becomes a ripening grape,

he will cut off the shoots with pruning knives,

and cut down and take away the spreading branches.

Isaiah 18:5

CHAPTER 7

First Fruits

First Fruits

o ···

Write Psalm 107:36-37 in the space below.

....

....

....

....

....

....

....

....

....

....

....

....

....

....

....

Record one word or phrase that stands out to you.

....

....

....

....

What might God be saying to me?

....

....

....

....

....

....

....

....

....

....

What might God be telling me to do?

....

....

....

....

....

....

....

....

....

....

PRAYER

Write a prayer thanking God for giving your life meaning and purpose. Ask Him to show you how you can serve Him today.

Write Proverbs 3:9-10 in the space below.

Record one word or phrase that stands out to you.

First Fruits

What might God be saying to me?

....
....
....
....
....
....
....
....
....
....

What might God be telling me to do?

....
....
....
....
....
....
....
....
....

PRAYER

Prayer Prompt

First Fruits

Read Psalm 27.

Record one word or phrase that stands out to you.

....

....

....

....

What might God be saying to me?

....

....

....

....

....

....

....

What might God be telling me to do?

....

....

....

....

....

....

PRAYER

Write a prayer asking the Lord to help you desire Him above all else.

First Fruits

Read luke 13:20-21.

Record one word or phrase that stands out to you.

....

....

....

....

What might God be saying to me?

....

....

....

....

....

....

....

What might God be telling me to do?

....

....

....

....

....

....

....

PRAYER

Ask the Lord to reveal to you how you can make a positive impact for His kingdom in the world around you today. Record your thoughts below.

First Fruits

Read 1 Samuel 16:1-13.

Record one word or phrase that stands out to you.

....

....

....

....

What might God be saying to me?

....

....

....

....

....

....

....

What might God be telling me to do?

....

....

....

....

....

....

PRAYER

Write a prayer asking God to anoint you powerfully with the Holy Spirit.

First Fruits

Ask the Lord to reveal to you what He has anointed you to do at this time in your life. Sit quietly and listen for his gentle whisper. Record your thoughts in the space below.

LIVING A LIFE OF PURPOSE

Then the Lord said, "Rise and anoint him; this is the one."

1 Samuel 16:12

THOUGHTS

....

....

....

....

....

....

....

....

....

....

QUESTIONS

....

....

....

....

....

....

....

....

....

....

PREPARE
to *share*

FAVORITES

....

....

....

....

....

....

....

....

....

....

PRAYER NEEDS

....

....

....

....

....

....

....

....

....

....

TWO ARE BETTER
than ONE

PRAYER

Write a prayer for your small group, Sunday school class or our online community. Ask that the Lord be honored through your conversation and fellowship time together.

REST & REFLECT

A verse to meditate on this week: But seek first his kingdom and

his righteousness, and all these things will be given to you as

well. Matthew 6:33

First Fruits

1. What does it mean to honor God with the first fruits of all your crops? Why do you think He asks this of us?

2. What is the one thing David seeks from the Lord? (Psalm 27)

3. What is David confident of? (Psalm 27)

4. What do you think the Parable of the Leaven (Yeast) means?

5. Why did the Lord choose David as the next king of Israel?

6 . What do you think it means to have the Holy Spirit come upon a person powerfully?

7. Is God still doing this today?

8. In what ways have you said 'yes' to God this week? How did you hear His voice? What was your response?

Very truly I tell you, whoever believes in me will do the works I have been doing, and they will do even greater things than these, because I am going to the Father.

John 14:12

CHAPTER 8

Preparing for Harvest

Preparing for Harvest

Write 2 Corinthians 9:6 in the space below.

....

....

....

....

....

....

....

....

....

....

....

....

....

....

....

Record one word or phrase that stands out to you.

....

....

....

....

What might God be saying to me?

....
....
....
....
....
....
....
....
....
....

What might God be telling me to do?

....
....
....
....
....
....
....
....
....

Preparing for Harvest

PRAYER

Ask the Lord to help you understand how you can sow generously for His kingdom today. Sit quietly and listen for His response for a moment. Record your thoughts below.

Write Proverbs 11:24-25 in the space below.

Record one word or phrase that stands out to you.

Preparing for Harvest

What might God be saying to me?

···
···
···
···
···
···
···
···
···
···

What might God be telling me to do?

···
···
···
···
···
···
···
···
···

PRAYER

Ask the Father to reveal to you someone whose soul you can refresh today. Ask Him to help you have the courage and strength to accomplish this task.

Preparing for Harvest

Read Psalm 128.

Record one word or phrase that stands out to you.

....

....

....

....

What might God be saying to me?

....

....

....

....

....

....

....

What might God be telling me to do?

....

....

....

....

....

....

....

PRAYER

Write a prayer of thanksgiving and praise to the Lord. Ask Him to help you live a life of obedience to His voice.

Preparing for Harvest

Read Matthew 13:24-30; 36-43.

Record one word or phrase that stands out to you.

....

....

....

....

What might God be saying to me?

....

....

....

....

....

....

....

What might God be telling me to do?

....

....

....

....

....

....

PRAYER

Ask the Father to give you ears to hear. Record any thoughts He lays on your heart.

Preparing for Harvest

Read Matthew 9:35-38; Acts 2:14-21.

Record one word or phrase that stands out to you.

....

....

....

....

What might God be saying to me?

....

....

....

....

....

....

....

What might God be telling me to do?

....

....

....

....

....

....

PRAYER

Write a prayer thanking God for pouring out His Spirit on you. Ask Him to help you be a powerful, productive worker in His harvest field.

Preparing for Harvest

Review all of the Living a Life of Purpose pages from previous weeks. Ask God to show you 5-10 specific things

you can do to make a difference for His kingdom. List them below. Pray over each item, then start taking action.

LIVING A LIFE OF PURPOSE

Day Five

In the last days, God says,

I will pour out my Spirit on all people.

Acts 2:17

THOUGHTS

....
....
....
....
....
....
....
....
....
....
....

QUESTIONS

....
....
....
....
....
....
....
....
....
....
....

PREPARE
to share

FAVORITES

....
....
....
....
....
....
....
....
....
....
....

PRAYER NEEDS

....
....
....
....
....
....
....
....
....
....
....

TWO ARE BETTER
than ONE

PRAYER

Write a prayer for your small group, Sunday school class or our online community. Ask that the Lord be honored through your conversation and fellowship time together.

....

....

....

....

....

....

....

....

....

....

....

....

....

....

....

....

REST & REFLECT

A verse to meditate on this week: I saw heaven standing open and there before me was a white horse, whose rider is called Faithful and True. With justice he judges and wages war. Revelation 19:11

Preparing for Harvest

Suggested Flow: Opening Prayer, Read Scripture, Review Prepare to Share Notes, Watch Video, Discuss Questions, Closing Prayer

1. What does sowing generously look like for you?

2. How is refreshing another person's soul a sign of spiritual maturity?

3. What is promised to those who obey God in Psalm 128?

4. In the Parable of the Wheat and Tares (Weeds) why does the farmer allow the weeds to grow?

5. How does this apply to your personal view of people who choose to live ungodly lives?

6 . What does Jesus tell His disciples to do in Matthew 9:38?

7. How does having God's spirit poured out on us change the way we live?

8. In what ways have you said 'yes' to God this week? How did you hear His voice? What was your response?

Thank You

Before you go, I'd like to say thank you for taking this journey through Scripture with me. I know your time is valuable and there are many Bible study resources available to you. I am both honored and humbled that you chose to spend your most valuable time of the day with one of my resources.

If you enjoyed this Bible Reading Plan and Prayer Journal, I could really use your help. Please take a minute to write a review on Amazon or recommend this study to a friend. Your feedback and encouragement help me to create the kind of Bible study resources that encourage your spiritual growth and intimate relationship with God.

For more free Bible study resources please visit my online women's Bible study community at BeautifulBibleStudies.com.

Made in the USA
Monee, IL
26 May 2022

97076133R00103